IN ASSOCIATION WITH

SQA

Hodder Gibson
Model Practice
Papers
WITH ANSWERS

PLUS: Official SQA Specimen Paper &
2014 Past Paper With Answers

National 5
Drama

2013 Specimen Question Paper,
Model Papers & 2014 Exam

HODDER
GIBSON
AN HACHETTE UK COMPANY

This book contains the official 2013 SQA Specimen Question Paper and 2014 Exam for National 5 Drama, with associated SQA approved answers modified from the official marking instructions that accompany the paper.

In addition the book contains model practice papers, together with answers, plus study skills advice. These papers, some of which may include a limited number of previously published SQA questions, have been specially commissioned by Hodder Gibson, and have been written by experienced senior teachers and examiners in line with the new National 5 syllabus and assessment outlines, Spring 2013. This is not SQA material but has been devised to provide further practice for National 5 examinations in 2014 and beyond.

Hodder Gibson is grateful to the copyright holders, as credited on the final page of the Answer Section, for permission to use their material. Every effort has been made to trace the copyright holders and to obtain their permission for the use of copyright material. Hodder Gibson will be happy to receive information allowing us to rectify any error or omission in future editions.

Hachette UK's policy is to use papers that are natural, renewable and recyclable products and made from wood grown in sustainable forests. The logging and manufacturing processes are expected to conform to the environmental regulations of the country of origin.

Orders: please contact Bookpoint Ltd, 130 Park Drive, Abingdon, Oxon OX14 4SE. Telephone: (44) 01235 827720. Fax: (44) 01235 400454. Lines are open 9.00–5.00, Monday to Saturday, with a 24-hour message answering service. Visit our website at www.hoddereducation.co.uk. Hodder Gibson can be contacted direct on: Tel: 0141 848 1609; Fax: 0141 889 6315; email: hoddergibson@hodder.co.uk

This collection first published in 2014 by
Hodder Gibson, an imprint of Hodder Education,
An Hachette UK Company
2a Christie Street
Paisley PA1 1NB

ʒBrightRED Hodder Gibson is grateful to Bright Red Publishing Ltd for collaborative work in preparation of this book and all SQA Past Paper, National 5 and Higher for CfE Model Paper titles 2014.

Typeset by PDQ Digital Media Solutions Ltd, Bungay, Suffolk NR35 1BY

Printed in the UK

A catalogue record for this title is available from the British Library

ISBN: 978-1-4718-3700-5

3 2 1

2015 2014

Introduction
Study Skills – what you need to know to pass exams!

Pause for thought

Many students might skip quickly through a page like this. After all, we all know how to revise. Do you really though?

Think about this:

"IF YOU ALWAYS DO WHAT YOU ALWAYS DO, YOU WILL ALWAYS GET WHAT YOU HAVE ALWAYS GOT."

Do you like the grades you get? Do you want to do better? If you get full marks in your assessment, then that's great! Change nothing! This section is just to help you get that little bit better than you already are.

There are two main parts to the advice on offer here. The first part highlights fairly obvious things but which are also very important. The second part makes suggestions about revision that you might not have thought about but which WILL help you.

Part 1

DOH! It's so obvious but …

Start revising in good time

Don't leave it until the last minute – this will make you panic.

Make a revision timetable that sets out work time AND play time.

Sleep and eat!

Obvious really, and very helpful. Avoid arguments or stressful things too – even games that wind you up. You need to be fit, awake and focused!

Know your place!

Make sure you know exactly **WHEN and WHERE** your exams are.

Know your enemy!

Make sure you know what to expect in the exam.

How is the paper structured?

How much time is there for each question?

What types of question are involved?

Which topics seem to come up time and time again?

Which topics are your strongest and which are your weakest?

Are all topics compulsory or are there choices?

Learn by DOING!

There is no substitute for past papers and practice papers – they are simply essential! Tackling this collection of papers and answers is exactly the right thing to be doing as your exams approach.

Part 2

People learn in different ways. Some like low light, some bright. Some like early morning, some like evening / night. Some prefer warm, some prefer cold. But everyone uses their BRAIN and the brain works when it is active. Passive learning – sitting gazing at notes – is the most INEFFICIENT way to learn anything. Below you will find tips and ideas for making your revision more effective and maybe even more enjoyable. What follows gets your brain active, and active learning works!

Activity 1 – Stop and review

Step 1

When you have done no more than 5 minutes of revision reading STOP!

Step 2

Write a heading in your own words which sums up the topic you have been revising.

Step 3

Write a summary of what you have revised in no more than two sentences. Don't fool yourself by saying, "I know it, but I cannot put it into words". That just means you don't know it well enough. If you cannot write your summary, revise that section again, knowing that you must write a summary at the end of it. Many of you will have notebooks full of blue/black ink writing. Many of the pages will not be especially attractive or memorable so try to liven them up a bit with colour as you are reviewing and rewriting. **This is a great memory aid, and memory is the most important thing.**

Activity 2 — Use technology!

Why should everything be written down? Have you thought about "mental" maps, diagrams, cartoons and colour to help you learn? And rather than write down notes, why not record your revision material?

What about having a text message revision session with friends? Keep in touch with them to find out how and what they are revising and share ideas and questions.

Why not make a video diary where you tell the camera what you are doing, what you think you have learned and what you still have to do? No one has to see or hear it, but the process of having to organise your thoughts in a formal way to explain something is a very important learning practice.

Be sure to make use of electronic files. You could begin to summarise your class notes. Your typing might be slow, but it will get faster and the typed notes will be easier to read than the scribbles in your class notes. Try to add different fonts and colours to make your work stand out. You can easily Google relevant pictures, cartoons and diagrams which you can copy and paste to make your work more attractive and **MEMORABLE**.

Activity 3 – This is it. Do this and you will know lots!

Step 1

In this task you must be very honest with yourself! Find the SQA syllabus for your subject (www.sqa.org.uk). Look at how it is broken down into main topics called MANDATORY knowledge. That means stuff you MUST know.

Step 2

BEFORE you do ANY revision on this topic, write a list of everything that you already know about the subject. It might be quite a long list but you only need to write it once. It shows you all the information that is already in your long-term memory so you know what parts you do not need to revise!

Step 3

Pick a chapter or section from your book or revision notes. Choose a fairly large section or a whole chapter to get the most out of this activity.

With a buddy, use Skype, Facetime, Twitter or any other communication you have, to play the game "If this is the answer, what is the question?". For example, if you are revising Geography and the answer you provide is "meander", your buddy would have to make up a question like "What is the word that describes a feature of a river where it flows slowly and bends often from side to side?".

Make up 10 "answers" based on the content of the chapter or section you are using. Give this to your buddy to solve while you solve theirs.

Step 4

Construct a wordsearch of at least 10 X 10 squares. You can make it as big as you like but keep it realistic. Work together with a group of friends. Many apps allow you to make wordsearch puzzles online. The words and phrases can go in any direction and phrases can be split. Your puzzle must only contain facts linked to the topic you are revising. Your task is to find 10 bits of information to hide in your puzzle, but you must not repeat information that you used in Step 3. DO NOT show where the words are. Fill up empty squares with random letters. Remember to keep a note of where your answers are hidden but do not show your friends. When you have a complete puzzle, exchange it with a friend to solve each other's puzzle.

Step 5

Now make up 10 questions (not "answers" this time) based on the same chapter used in the previous two tasks. Again, you must find NEW information that you have not yet used. Now it's getting hard to find that new information! Again, give your questions to a friend to answer.

Step 6

As you have been doing the puzzles, your brain has been actively searching for new information. Now write a NEW LIST that contains only the new information you have discovered when doing the puzzles. Your new list is the one to look at repeatedly for short bursts over the next few days. Try to remember more and more of it without looking at it. After a few days, you should be able to add words from your second list to your first list as you increase the information in your long-term memory.

FINALLY! Be inspired...

Make a list of different revision ideas and beside each one write **THINGS I HAVE** tried, **THINGS I WILL** try and **THINGS I MIGHT** try. Don't be scared of trying something new.

And remember – "FAIL TO PREPARE AND PREPARE TO FAIL!"

National 5 Drama

The course

In the National 5 Drama course you will have had the opportunity to contribute to the creation of drama based on stimuli or text. You will also have had the option of working as an actor or in a production role.

The practical component is worth 60 marks, which are split as follows:

- 10 marks for the Preparation for Performance Brief
- 50 marks for the Performance Exam

The written part of the course is worth 40 marks for which these model papers give practice.

The exam

Section 1

Section 1 of the examination paper is worth 10 marks and you can answer from the point of view of an acting or production role (set, costume, make-up and hair, props and set dressing, lighting, sound).

In the question paper you will firstly have to answer questions based on a performance you have taken part in during the course. This may be from any unit and for any skill. The basis of your answers will be an evaluation of the preparation you undertook and the final performance. You should try to give as much detail as possible and, when asked, give reasons for your answers. Many candidates lose marks by not giving a full enough evaluation, so think about the strengths and weaknesses of your drama from every angle so you can write about how well it worked or how it could have been improved.

You should make sure you use appropriate, correct terminology for all questions. If the terminology you use is vague, you will lose marks. You should make sure you can discuss, evaluate and explain all aspects of the drama you have chosen to write about. Think about the list below:

Characterisation – practical drama techniques you used to create characters, including rehearsal techniques.

Performance or design concepts – concepts you created to enhance your drama. This may be in relation to target audience, mood and atmosphere, setting, genre, theme etc. Appropriate terminology should be used for the production skill being discussed.

Styles/genre of your drama – identify the style or genre of your drama (comedy, tragedy, western, tragicomedy).

Setting – where and when your drama is set.

Staging/venue – what venue, staging and set design you would use in order to make clear this setting.

Themes/issues and message – what are the themes/issues of your drama? You may also be asked to identify and justify dramatic message.

Voice and movement terminology – terminology must be used when discussing the performance of a character or the presentation of a key moment.

Mood and atmosphere – you must be able to explain the mood and atmosphere of your drama.

Target audience – you must be able to identify, justify and discuss the target audience's reaction to your drama.

Section 2

Section 2 of your examination is worth 30 marks. It is based on your response to three unseen stimuli. You will have to choose **one** of the stimuli to develop ideas for a drama and your answers will be based on a piece of drama that could be created and performed to an audience.

The stimulus in Section 2 may be a picture, extract from a text, extract from a novel, poem, phrase, quote, newspaper headline etc. You will choose the one that you think you could create the best drama from.

In this part of the paper you will be given a blank page. This page is for you to make any notes, mind maps, lists, diagrams that help you with your ideas. This page will **not** be marked.

Although you may not be asked to write the plot of your drama you will need to have worked out your storyline. This is crucial as you will have to be able to answer questions that relate to the drama you would want to create. Questions may refer to characters, rehearsal techniques, mood and atmosphere, style, genre, staging, setting, venues, target audience, key moments, performance and design concepts and themes and issues. You will also be given a page at the end of the paper for you to draw any diagrams to exemplify or support your answers.

Candidates often lose marks as they contradict themselves. Make sure that later answers don't conflict with previous ones, as this will lead to you losing marks.

Questions are often linked so it is essential that you read all the questions first. This will ensure that you are answering the question set and can answer further questions that are related.

Again in Section 2, details and full explanations are expected. Imagine you are painting a picture with words for your examiner to help them understand your ideas and concepts. Make sure ideas are achievable; for example, in lighting and sound responses, you need to be aware of how your ideas will look and sound to an audience. Loud effects/music or flashing colour changes in lighting are not practical when they occur during dialogue and will merely distract from the action.

It is also important that you give **reasons** for your answers. Many candidates give a description of what they do but fail to give reasons why. If a questions asks for reasons, you will be awarded marks for these, and missing out justification will lead to you losing marks.

For example, you may have stated that you want a calm and peaceful mood and atmosphere at the end of your drama. Later on in the paper you might describe that to create this mood and atmosphere you would use a red/orange wash of lighting. Red and orange are not traditionally colours used for this mood and atmosphere, but you state that at the end of your drama the issues from your drama have been resolved and your lighting is to signify the two main characters sitting together peacefully watching the sunset. This explains the reason for this choice and would gain marks.

Appropriate, correct terminology is expected for all your answers. If terminology used is vague you will lose marks.

Good luck!

Remember that the rewards for passing National 5 Drama are well worth it! Your pass will help you get the future you want for yourself. In the exam, be confident in your own ability. If you're not sure how to answer a question, trust your instincts and just give it a go anyway – keep calm and don't panic!

NATIONAL 5

2013 Specimen
Question Paper

N5

National Qualifications
SPECIMEN ONLY

Mark

SQ10/N5/01

Drama

Date — Not applicable

Duration — 1 hour and 30 mins

Fill in these boxes and read what is printed below.

Full name of centre

Town

Forename(s)

Surname

Number of seat

Date of birth

Day   Month   Year

D D   M M   Y Y

Scottish candidate number

Total marks — 40

SECTION 1 — 10 marks

Attempt ALL the questions based on a performance you have taken part in during the Drama course.

SECTION 2 — 30 marks

Select from the stimuli and attempt ALL the questions based on the chosen stimulus.

You may use sketches/drawings to illustrate your answers.

Write your answers clearly, in **blue** or **black** ink, in the spaces provided.

Before leaving the examination room you must give this booklet to the Invigilator.
If you do not, you may lose all the marks for this paper.

MARKS | DO NOT WRITE IN THIS MARGIN

SECTION 1 — 10 marks

Consider a performance you have taken part in during your course as either an actor or in a production role.

Tick the box to indicate your role.

Actor ☐   Lighting ☐   Costume ☐   Set ☐

Props and set dressing ☐   Sound ☐   Make-up and hair ☐

1. (a) Who would be the ideal target audience for your drama?

    Explain your answer.   2

    _____

    _____

    _____

    _____

    _____

    _____

    (b) What range of emotions did you want the audience to feel when they were watching the performance?

    Explain your answer.   2

    _____

    _____

    _____

    _____

    _____

    Total marks   4

MARKS DO NOT WRITE IN THIS MARGIN

2. Evaluate the effectiveness of your final performance.

If you were **an actor** you should include comments on performance concepts and the mood/atmosphere created.

OR

If you were in a **production role** you should include comments on design concepts and the mood/atmosphere created.   6

_____

_____

_____

_____

_____

_____

_____

_____

_____

_____

_____

_____

_____

_____

_____

_____

_____

_____

_____

MARKS | DO NOT WRITE IN THIS MARGIN

SECTION 2 — 30 marks

Choose **one** of the following stimuli to develop ideas for a drama. Your answers should be based on a piece of drama which **could** be created and performed to an audience.

Stimulus A

Forbidden Love

Stimulus B

Where childhood memories go?

Stimulus C

Mum:	What the hell've you been up to?
Alex:	What did he say?
Mum:	He said you got fired yesterday.
Alex:	And?
Mum:	And! What d'you mean, 'and'?
Alex:	Did he say anything else?
Mum:	Something about castanets.
Alex:	Oh God!
Mum:	Have you been nicking stuff from your work?
Alex:	No.
Mum:	What's that then, a leaving present?
Alex:	Look...
Mum:	Look nothing. I'm not having the polis at my door because of you. If you've got yourself into trouble you can get yourself out of here. I've warned you, you can pack your bags and...
Mum:	Where are you going?
Alex:	Eh?
Mum:	Oh aye. Spain, is it? Costa del Crime n'that, eh?
Alex:	Spain!
Mum:	Castanets.
Alex:	No. Look. I just need to go away for a while. Trust me.
Mum:	About as far as I could throw you.
Alex:	It's fine.
Mum:	I'm not going through all that business again. D'you hear me?
Alex:	I hear you. I have to go.
Mum:	Just like his father.

Extract from: *PASSING PLACES* by Stephen Greenhorn

Tick (✓) the appropriate box to indicate which stimulus you have chosen to write about.

Stimulus A ☐   Stimulus B ☐   Stimulus C ☐

You should now READ ALL of the following Questions 3a–5b to guide your answers on your chosen stimulus.

You may use drawings and/or diagrams to illustrate any of your answers if you wish.

The space below is provided for any rough working and **will not** be marked.

MARKS

3. (a) Describe a time period in which you would choose to set your drama and explain your choice.

2

_____

_____

_____

_____

_____

_____

(b) Think about the purpose or message of your drama. How will the plot and setting help to communicate this purpose or message?

6

_____

_____

_____

_____

_____

_____

_____

_____

_____

_____

_____

_____

_____

_____

_____

_____

3. **(continued)**

(c) Name **two** conventions you would use in your drama and, for each one, explain the **advantage** of using it.   **4**

_____

_____

_____

_____

_____

_____

_____

_____

_____

_____

_____

_____

Total marks 12

4. (a) As an actor, consider a character in your drama who you think would be a challenge to portray and explain why.   **2**

_____

_____

_____

_____

_____

_____

4. (continued)

(b) Describe the relationship **this character** has with **one other character** in your drama.

2

_____

_____

_____

_____

_____

_____

(c) Describe **two rehearsal activities** that could help establish and/or develop the relationship you have just described, and explain why these would be helpful.

4

_____

_____

_____

_____

_____

_____

_____

_____

_____

_____

_____

_____

_____

Total marks   8

MARKS | DO NOT WRITE IN THIS MARGIN

5. (a) Choose and describe a **key moment** in your drama. Explain why you consider it to be a key moment.

4

_____

_____

_____

_____

_____

_____

_____

_____

_____

_____

_____

MARKS | DO NOT WRITE IN THIS MARGIN

5. (continued)

(b) Think again about that key moment. As a **designer**, how would you use two production areas to highlight/enhance this key moment? Give **reasons** for each production area you have chosen. A blank page is provided for any drawings/diagrams.   **6**

_____

_____

_____

_____

_____

_____

_____

_____

_____

_____

_____

_____

_____

_____

_____

_____

_____

Total marks   10

Use this page for any drawings/diagrams.

[END OF SPECIMEN QUESTION PAPER]

Acknowledgement of Copyright

Section 2 Stimulus B   Image entitled "Where childhood memories go?" by Carlos Chacon from
                        www.Charlie.cr.smugmug.com. Reproduced by kind permission of Carlos Chacon.

Section 2 Stimulus C   Extract is taken from the play "Passing Places" by Stephen Greenhorn taken from
                        "Scotland Plays" ISBN: 1854593838. Reproduced by permission of Nick Hern Books
                        Ltd.

Model Paper 1

Whilst this Model Practice Paper has been specially commissioned by Hodder Gibson for use as practice for the National 5 exams, the key reference documents remain the SQA Specimen Paper 2013 and the SQA Past Paper 2014.

National
Qualifications
MODEL PAPER 1

Drama

Duration — 1 hour and 30 minutes

Total marks — 40

SECTION 1 — 10 marks

Attempt ALL the questions based on a performance you have taken part in during the Drama course.

SECTION 2 — 30 marks

Select from the stimuli and attempt ALL questions based on the chosen stimulus.

You may use sketches/drawings to illustrate your answers.

Write your answers clearly, in **blue** or **black** ink, in the spaces provided.

SECTION 1 — 10 marks

Consider a performance you have taken part in during your course as either an actor or in a production role.

Tick the box to indicate your role.

Actor ☐   Lighting ☐   Costume ☐   Set ☐

Props and set dressing ☐   Sound ☐   Make-up and hair ☐

1.   (a)   Describe the main problem you had when preparing your drama.   **2**

_____

_____

_____

_____

_____

_____

(b)   Explain how you solved this problem.   **2**

_____

_____

_____

_____

_____

_____

_____

_____

Total marks   4

MARKS

2. Evaluate the effectiveness of your final performance.

If you were **an actor** you should include comments on performance concepts and impact on the audience.

OR

If you were in a **production role** you should include comments on design concepts and impact on the audience.

6

_____

_____

_____

_____

_____

_____

_____

_____

_____

_____

_____

_____

_____

_____

_____

_____

_____

_____

_____

SECTION 2 — 30 marks

Choose **one** of the following stimuli to develop ideas for a drama. Your answers should be based on a piece of drama which **could** be created and performed to an audience.

Stimulus A

No one in Scotland can escape from the past.
It is everywhere, haunting like a ghost.

Scottish saying by Geddes MacGregor

Stimulus B

In Sickness and in Health

Stimulus C

As grit swirls in the wind the word spreads.
On pavements approaching the bridge a crowd
Springs up like mushrooms.
They are hushed at first, intently

Looking. At the top of the pylon
The target of their gaze leans toward them.
The sky sobs
With the sirens of disaster crews

Careening toward the crowd with nets,
Ladders, resuscitation gear, their First
Aid attendants antiseptic in white duck.
The police, strapped into their holsters,

Exert themselves in crowd-control. They can't
Control the situation.
Atop the pylon there's a man who threatens
Violence. He shouts...........

Excerpt from: *THE CENTER OF ATTENTION* by Daniel Hoffman

MARKS

Tick (✓) the appropriate box to indicate which stimulus you have chosen to write about.

Stimulus A ☐   Stimulus B ☐   Stimulus C ☐

You should now READ ALL of the following Questions 3a-5b to guide your answers on your chosen stimulus.

You may use drawings and/or diagrams to illustrate any of your answers if you wish.

The space below is provided for any rough working and **will not** be marked.

3. (a) Who would you consider a suitable target audience for your drama? Give reasons for your answer.

2

_____

_____

_____

_____

_____

_____

(b) What emotional reaction(s) do you think this audience would have when watching your drama?

4

_____

_____

_____

_____

_____

_____

_____

_____

_____

_____

_____

_____

_____

Total marks   6

MARKS

4. (a) Outline a character from your drama who you want your target audience to feel strongly about.

Justify why you have chosen this character.　　2

_____

_____

_____

_____

_____

_____

(b) Explain why you think your target audience would react strongly to this character. Your explanations could refer to personality, purpose in the drama, relationships with other characters, status etc. **You should justify your answer.**　　4

_____

_____

_____

_____

_____

_____

_____

_____

_____

_____

_____

_____

_____

_____

Total marks　6

5. (a) Choose and describe an **important moment** in your drama where this character appears. Explain why you consider it to be an important moment for this character.   4

_____

_____

_____

_____

_____

_____

_____

_____

_____

_____

5. (a) Choose and describe an **important moment** in your drama where this character appears. Explain why you consider it to be an important moment for this character.

MARKS | DO NOT WRITE IN THIS MARGIN

5. **(continued)**

(b) As a **designer**, explain how you would use **at least two production areas** to emphasise this important moment? Give **reasons** for each production area you have chosen. A blank page is provided for any drawings/diagrams.   **6**

_____

_____

_____

_____

_____

_____

_____

_____

_____

_____

_____

_____

_____

_____

_____

_____

_____

_____

Total marks 10

MARKS | DO NOT WRITE IN THIS MARGIN

6. (a) Choose **one** other character from your drama who has a low status. Outline the main purpose of this character.   **2**

_____

_____

_____

_____

_____

_____

(b) As a **director**, explain how you would want an actor to use voice in order to portray this character's low status.   **3**

_____

_____

_____

_____

_____

_____

(c) As a **director**, explain how you would want an actor to use movement in order to portray his character's low status.   **3**

_____

_____

_____

_____

_____

_____

Total marks   **8**

MARKS | DO NOT WRITE IN THIS MARGIN

Use this page for any drawings/diagrams.

[END OF MODEL QUESTION PAPER]

Model Paper 2

Whilst this Model Practice Paper has been specially commissioned by Hodder Gibson for use as practice for the National 5 exams, the key reference documents remain the SQA Specimen Paper 2013 and the SQA Past Paper 2014.

HODDER GIBSON
LEARN MORE

National Qualifications
MODEL PAPER 2

Drama

Duration — 1 hour and 30 minutes

Total marks — 40

SECTION 1 — 10 marks

Attempt ALL the questions based on a performance you have taken part in during the Drama course.

SECTION 2 — 30 marks

Select from the stimuli and attempt ALL questions based on the chosen stimulus.

You may use sketches/drawings to illustrate your answers.

Write your answers clearly, in **blue** or **black** ink, in the spaces provided.

SECTION 1 — 10 marks

Consider a performance you have taken part in during your course as either an actor or in a production role.

Tick the box to indicate your role.

Actor ☐   **Lighting** ☐   Costume ☐   Set ☐

Props and set dressing ☐   Sound ☐   **Make-up and hair** ☐

1. If you had been given the choice between the target audiences below, which would you have chosen? Justify your answer.

   11- to 16-year-olds   **OR**   20- to 30-year-olds   **2**

   _____

   _____

   _____

   _____

   _____

   _____

2. Describe **two** problems which you encountered when preparing for this performance. What solution did you find for each problem?   **4**

   _____

   _____

   _____

   _____

   _____

   _____

   _____

   _____

MARKS

3. Consider your final performance. Describe **two** changes you would make in relation to your contribution.

   If you were **an actor** you should include comments on performance concepts.

   OR

   If you were in a **production role** you should include comments on design concepts.

4

_____

_____

_____

_____

_____

_____

_____

_____

_____

_____

_____

_____

_____

_____

_____

_____

_____

_____

SECTION 2 — 30 marks

Choose one of the following stimuli to develop ideas for a drama. Your answers should be based on a piece of drama which **could** be created and performed to an audience.

Stimulus A

Stimulus B

She has no sense at all of the tension that has caught the little clutch of peat cutters ahead of her. No way, from her limited experience, of reading the body language of the men crouched down around the stretch of trench wall that has collapsed about their feet.

Too late her father sees her coming and shouts at her to stay back. Too late for her to stop her forward momentum, or respond to the panic in his voice. The men stand suddenly, turning towards her, and she sees her brother's face the colour of cotton sheets laid out in the sun to bleach.

And she follows his eyes down to the fallen peat bank and the arm that lies stretched out towards her, leathery skin like brown parchment, fingers curled as if holding an invisible ball. One leg lies twisted over the other, a head tipped towards the ditch as if in search of a lost life, black holes where the eyes should have been.

For a moment she is lost in a sea of incomprehension, before realisation washes over her, and the scream is whipped from her mouth by the wind.

Extract from: *THE LEWIS MAN* by Peter May

Stimulus C

Buzz: I'm Buzz.

Speed: I'm Speed.

Russell: Don't get touchy now, you two—Lift him!

Jake: Nooooo!

Polly: Stop!

Carol: Stop!

Natasha: You're gonna really hurt him.

Russell: Trying my best.

Natasha: Shane!

Polly: But you can't! Please! He... he was telling us a story. Wasn't he, Tasha?

Natasha: ... What? Oh... yeah! A good story.

Polly: And we want to know how it ends.

Russell: I hate stories.

Jake: Help! Help!

Natasha: Shane! Tell him! Please!

Slight pause.

Russell: What's it to be, Shane? Dangle or story?

Pause.

Shane: ... Story.

Russell: But, Shane—

Natasha: You heard!

Extract from *SPARKLESHARK* by Philip Ridley

DO NOT
WRITE IN
THIS
MARGIN

Tick (✓) the appropriate box to indicate which stimulus you have chosen to write about.

Stimulus A ☐   Stimulus B ☐   Stimulus C ☐

You should now READ ALL of the following Questions 4–7b to guide your answers on your chosen stimulus.

You may use drawings and/or diagrams to illustrate any of your answers if you wish.

The space below is provided for any rough working and **will not** be marked.

MARKS | DO NOT WRITE IN THIS MARGIN

4. Give a brief outline of your drama indicating any changes to time and place.   **4**

_____

_____

_____

_____

_____

_____

_____

_____

_____

_____

5. (a) What mood and atmosphere would you want to create in your opening scene of your drama? Give reasons for your choice.   **4**

Mood and atmosphere _____

_____

_____

_____

_____

_____

_____

_____

_____

_____

_____

5. (continued)

(b) Think about **two** production areas that could help establish this mood and atmosphere.

Describe how each production area could help achieve the mood/ atmosphere you would wish to create.

6

Production skill 1: _____

_____

_____

_____

_____

_____

_____

_____

Production skill 2: _____

_____

_____

_____

_____

_____

_____

_____

_____

_____

Total marks 10

MARKS | DO NOT WRITE IN THIS MARGIN

6. (a) "Conflict and tension are the essence of drama."

Describe what the conflict and/or tension would be in your drama.   **2**

_____

_____

_____

_____

_____

_____

(b) As a **director**, in what ways could you help your actors understand this conflict and/or tension in rehearsal?   **4**

_____

_____

_____

_____

_____

_____

_____

_____

_____

_____

_____

Total marks   6

MARKS | DO NOT WRITE IN THIS MARGIN

7. (a) Choose **one** character from your drama. Outline this character's **personality** and overall **purpose** in the drama.   4

_____

_____

_____

_____

_____

_____

_____

_____

(b) If you were to act this character, how would you communicate this personality to an audience, making reference to a range of performance concepts.   6

_____

_____

_____

_____

_____

_____

_____

_____

_____

_____

_____

_____

Total marks 10

MARKS | DO NOT WRITE IN THIS MARGIN

Use this page for any drawings/diagrams.

[END OF MODEL QUESTION PAPER]

Model Paper 3

Whilst this Model Practice Paper has been specially commissioned by Hodder Gibson for use as practice for the National 5 exams, the key reference documents remain the SQA Specimen Paper 2013 and the SQA Past Paper 2014.

National
Qualifications
MODEL PAPER 3

Drama

Duration — 1 hour and 30 minutes

Total marks — 40

SECTION 1 — 10 marks

Attempt ALL the questions based on a performance you have taken part in during the Drama course.

SECTION 2 — 30 marks

Select from the stimuli and attempt ALL questions based on the chosen stimulus.

You may use sketches/drawings to illustrate your answers.

Write your answers clearly, in **blue** or **black** ink, in the spaces provided.

MARKS | DO NOT WRITE IN THIS MARGIN

SECTION 1 — 10 marks

Consider a performance you have taken part in during your course as either an actor or in a production role.

Tick the box to indicate your role.

Actor ☐   Lighting ☐   Costume ☐   Set ☐

Props and set dressing ☐   **Sound** ☐   **Make up and hair** ☐

1. Explain how your role improved the performance.   **2**

_____

_____

_____

_____

_____

_____

_____

2. How successful was your role? Justify your answer.   **2**

_____

_____

_____

_____

_____

_____

_____

_____

MARKS | DO NOT WRITE IN THIS MARGIN

3. Consider a moment in your final performance that created a strong impact with the audience.

Describe that strong impact and, if you were an **actor**, how you achieved this. You should include in your answer a range of performance concepts.

OR

Describe that strong impact and, if you were in a **production role**, how you achieved this. You should include in your answer a range of design concepts.   **6**

_____

_____

_____

_____

_____

_____

_____

_____

_____

_____

_____

_____

_____

_____

_____

_____

_____

_____

SECTION 2 — 30 marks

Choose **one** of the following stimuli to develop ideas for a drama. Your answers should be based on a piece of drama which **could** be created and performed to an audience.

Stimulus A

Stimulus B

Do good, reap good; do evil, reap evil.

Chinese proverb

MARKS | DO NOT WRITE IN THIS MARGIN

Stimulus C

Siward: Good to see you.

Macduff: Siward

Siward: What's your report?

Macduff: The tyrant is dead.

Siward: Good.

Macduff: He was running when we caught him.

A spear in his back.

They brought him to me on the hill above the wood.

He couldn't speak but I looked into his eyes and there

was still life there.

It was a pleasure to extinguish it.

I cut his throat.

His head's on a stick in the castle yard.

Siward: It's over.

Macduff: Yes.

Siward: Is there something else?

Macduff: Osborn.

Your son.

He was with the Cumbrians.

They were riding in pursuit through the forest.

Osborn was riding at the front. He was with the leaders

moving through the woods. As they got near one of the

Scots lords turned suddenly and shot a bolt.

It must have been a lucky shot.

Through the trees like that.

Shooting as they ran.

Luck.

Siward: Osborn is dead.

Macduff: I'm sorry.

Extract from **DUNSINANE** by David Greig

Tick (✓) the appropriate box to indicate which stimulus you have chosen to write about.

Stimulus A ☐   Stimulus B ☐   Stimulus C ☐

You should now READ ALL of the following Questions 4–8 to guide your answers on your chosen stimulus.

You may use drawings and/or diagrams to illustrate any of your answers if you wish.

The space below is provided for any rough working and **will not** be marked.

4. What form would your drama take?

1

_____

_____

_____

_____

_____

5. (a) Describe in detail the set the audience would see as your drama starts.

4

_____

_____

_____

_____

_____

_____

_____

_____

_____

_____

_____

_____

_____

_____

MARKS

DO NOT WRITE IN THIS MARGIN

5. (continued)

(b) How might you use theatre arts to make the set clear and interesting for an audience?

You should give a detailed explanation of how you could use **at least two** theatre arts from the following list:

6

- Lighting
- Sound
- Props
- Set dressings

Justify your answer.

_____

_____

_____

_____

_____

_____

_____

_____

_____

_____

_____

_____

_____

_____

Total marks 10

MARKS | DO NOT WRITE IN THIS MARGIN

6. (a) Think about the main character in your drama. Describe this character's purpose in the drama.

2

_____

_____

_____

_____

_____

_____

(b) In what ways would you show an audience that this was the main character? You may wish to consider acting techniques, theatre arts, status etc.

6

_____

_____

_____

_____

_____

_____

_____

_____

_____

_____

_____

_____

Total marks **8**

MARKS | DO NOT WRITE IN THIS MARGIN

7. (a) The director decides to end your drama with a **tableau**. Describe how the end of your drama could be turned into a **tableau**.

3

_____

_____

_____

_____

_____

_____

_____

(b) Do you think a **tableau** at the end of your drama would be successful? **Justify your answer.**

2

_____

_____

_____

_____

_____

_____

_____

_____

_____

_____

_____

_____

Total marks 5

MARKS

8. As a **designer**, explain and justify how you would use **two** production areas to highlight your overall **genre** to an audience. A blank page is provided for any drawings/diagrams.

    6

_____

_____

_____

_____

_____

_____

_____

_____

_____

_____

_____

_____

_____

_____

_____

_____

_____

_____

_____

_____

_____

_____

_____

_____

Use this page for any drawings/diagrams.

[END OF MODEL QUESTION PAPER]

NATIONAL 5

2014

National Qualifications 2014

Mark

X721/75/01

Drama

THURSDAY, 15 MAY
9:00 AM – 10:30 AM

Fill in these boxes and read what is printed below.

Full name of centre

Town

Forename(s)

Surname

Number of seat

Date of birth

Day	Month	Year
D D	M M	Y Y

Scottish candidate number

Total marks — 40

SECTION 1 — 10 marks

Attempt ALL the questions based on a performance you have taken part in during the Drama course.

SECTION 2 — 30 marks

Select from the stimuli and attempt ALL the questions based on the chosen stimulus.

Write your answers clearly in the spaces provided in this booklet. Additional space for answers is provided at the end of this booklet. If you use this space, you must clearly identify the question number you are attempting.

Use **blue** or **black** ink.

Before leaving the examination room you must give this booklet to the Invigilator; if you do not, you may lose all the marks for this paper.

MARKS | DO NOT WRITE IN THIS MARGIN

SECTION 1 — 10 marks

Consider a performance you have taken part in during your Course as either an actor or in a production role.

Tick the box to indicate your role.

Actor [ ]   Lighting [ ]   Costume [ ]   Set [ ]

Props and set dressing [ ]   Sound [ ]   Make-up and hair [ ]

1. Choose the scene from your drama which you found most challenging.

    (a) Give a **brief** description of this scene.   **1**

    _____

    _____

    _____

    (b) Explain why you found this scene to be the most challenging.   **2**

    _____

    _____

    _____

    _____

    _____

    _____

MARKS

1. (continued)

(c)　What did you do to overcome the challenge?

2

_____

_____

_____

_____

_____

_____

_____

[Turn over

MARKS | DO NOT WRITE IN THIS MARGIN

1. (continued)

(d) In your role as actor or part of the technical team how did you ensure that this scene worked as well as possible in the final performance?

If you were an **actor** you should comment on characterisation and performance concepts.

OR

If you were in a **production role** you should include comments on the design concepts.

You may use sketches/drawings to illustrate your answer. (Use the space provided on the following page).

5

_____

_____

_____

_____

_____

_____

_____

_____

_____

_____

_____

_____

_____

_____

Total marks 10

MARKS

[Turn over

SECTION 2 — 30 marks

Choose **one** of the following stimuli to develop ideas for a drama. Your answers should be based on a piece of drama which **could** be created and performed to an audience.

Stimulus A

Stimulus B

Short extract from "Medea" by Liz Lochhead

That cry!
It was a cry we've heard
From the woman
Opening the door to the telegraph in wartime
The cry from the unquiet wife
Opening the door
To the chequered hats of two policemen
Late late on a foggy night
The cry from the mother in the hospital corridor
When she sees the doctor's face

Stimulus C

"Do not dwell in the past, do not dream of the future, concentrate the mind on the present moment".

Buddha

Tick (✓) the appropriate box to indicate which stimulus you have chosen to write about.

Stimulus A ☐   Stimulus B ☐   Stimulus C ☐

You should now READ ALL of the following Questions to guide your answers on your chosen stimulus.

The space below is provided for any rough working and **will not** be marked.

[Turn over

MARKS | DO NOT WRITE IN THIS MARGIN

2. Who would be the ideal target audience for your drama?

   Justify your answer.

   2

_____

_____

_____

_____

_____

_____

3. Explain in detail the drama which the audience would see.

   In your answer you may include form, conventions used, genre and style of the piece.

   4

_____

_____

_____

_____

_____

_____

_____

_____

_____

_____

_____

MARKS

4. (a) Identify what you would consider to be the main theme or issue of your drama.

1

_____

_____

_____

(b) Describe how you would develop this theme or issue in your drama.

2

_____

_____

_____

_____

_____

(c) Explain how you might highlight this theme or issue through character relationships.

Discuss at least two characters from your drama.

3

_____

_____

_____

_____

_____

_____

_____

Total marks 6

[Turn over

MARKS | DO NOT WRITE IN THIS MARGIN

5. (a) Choose any character from your drama. Explain this character's purpose in your drama.

2

_____

_____

_____

_____

_____

_____

(b) How does the character that you selected in Question 5(a) feel about **one** other character in your drama? Justify your answer.

4

_____

_____

_____

_____

_____

_____

_____

_____

_____

_____

_____

_____

_____

Total marks   6

MARKS

6. (a) Briefly describe a key moment in your drama. Explain your answer.　2

_____

_____

_____

_____

_____

_____

(b) As a director, in what ways would you direct the actors to use their voice **and** movement to help highlight this key moment?　4

_____

_____

_____

_____

_____

_____

_____

_____

_____

_____

_____

_____

_____

[Turn over for Question 6 (c) on *Page twelve*

MARKS | DO NOT WRITE IN THIS MARGIN

6. (continued)

(c) Which two production skills, from the list below, would you use to highlight the key moment you have discussed in Questions 6 (a) and 6 (b)?

Give reasons for your answer.

      Costume   **Make-up**   **Props**   **Lighting**   **6**

Production Skill 1 _____

_____

_____

_____

_____

_____

_____

Production Skill 2 _____

_____

_____

_____

_____

_____

_____

_____

Total marks 12

[END OF QUESTION PAPER]

MARKS | DO NOT WRITE IN THIS MARGIN

ADDITIONAL SPACE FOR ANSWERS

ADDITIONAL SPACE FOR ANSWERS

Acknowledgement of copyright

Stimulus A   Image from www.shutterstock.com

Stimulus B   Short extract from "Medea" by Liz Lochhead

SQA AND HODDER GIBSON NATIONAL 5 DRAMA 2014

NATIONAL 5 DRAMA
SPECIMEN QUESTION PAPER

Overview

National 5 level candidates are required to demonstrate knowledge and understanding of both process and performance.

Section A is designed to test the candidates' ability to evaluate their own and others' work. Section B tests the candidates' ability to respond to stimuli and create their own piece of drama.

Section 1

These questions require candidates to give a personal evaluative response to a piece of work they have been involved in during the course. This may be from the Drama Skills or Production Units or from the Course Assessment Performance.

The questions require candidates to demonstrate their reflection and evaluation skills.

Section 2

Candidates are required to demonstrate knowledge and understanding of creating drama by responding to stimuli. The questions should be suitable for candidates with a relatively detailed knowledge as well as those whose knowledge is more wide ranging.

Section 1

(a) Candidates are asked to state who the ideal target audience for the performance would be and to explain their choice.

One mark for identifying ideal target audience. Target audience is the group of people you intend to present to.

One mark for appropriate reason for target audience.

Candidates should be specific e.g. about age group, demographic, generation, certain group in society.

An appropriate reason would be one such as:

"An older audience (OAPs) would be ideal as the play was set in the 50s and they will relate to the period."

(b) The candidate is asked to comment on a range of emotions they wanted the audience to have when watching the presentation.

The candidate:

- Has made detailed and fully justified comments about how they wanted the audience to respond to the performance with appropriate emotional reaction –2 marks.

- Has given an adequate explanation, with some justification, about how they wanted the audience to respond to the performance with an appropriate emotional reaction – 1 mark.

Candidates should make direct reference to the text or specific concepts.

Quotations are acceptable.

2. Candidates are asked to evaluate their final performance.

Answer may include comments on:

Acting — performance concept, voice, movement, blocking, mood and atmosphere.

Lighting — design concept, mood and atmosphere, operation, use of resources.

Sound — design concept, mood and atmosphere, operation, use of resources.

Costume — design concept, effectiveness, use of resources.

Make-up — design concept, effectiveness, use of resources.

Set — design concept, effectiveness, use of resources.

Props — design concept, effectiveness, use of resources.

Any other evaluative comments referring to their performance should be awarded marks.

Section 2

3. (a) There are two marks for suggesting and justifying a time period to set the drama.

The candidate:

- Has clearly identified a time period and given full and relevant justification for that choice — 2 marks

- Has identified a time period and given some justification for that choice — 1 mark

A full justification will give two reasons for choice. Some justification would be one reason.

A variety of time period responses could be given i.e. the seventies, the late nineties, 1890, present day, 20 years in the future.

All are acceptable.

(b) Candidates should concisely write the plot for the piece of drama they would create, including its purpose or message, based on one of the stimuli given.

Six marks for plot of drama (must include time and place of action). Two marks will be awarded for time and place. Four marks will be awarded for plot of drama showing how this would communicate their purpose or message.

Candidates may choose to outline the whole plot of the drama or split into scenes. Whichever is chosen, the answer must be succinct. Either is acceptable as long as time and place are included. Candidates must include the purpose or message of their drama.

It must be appropriate for theatrical presentation.

(c) Candidates are asked to name two conventions. Each convention will have one mark for appropriate use and one mark for the advantage stated of that convention.

- narrator
- voice over
- freeze frame
- slow motion
- tableaux
- flashback
- flash forward
- thought tracking
- monologue

Any other conventions should be awarded marks.

EXAMPLE

Narrator
- helps to clarify action for audience
- can keep audience distanced from action
- can connect with audience, make them feel part of action
- give privileged information

Voice over
- tells audience how characters are feeling
- useful for establishing time/location or imparting information

Freeze frame
- highlights important parts of the play

4. (a) Candidates are asked to explain, with reasons, which character would be a challenge to portray in their drama.

The candidate:

- Has clearly identified the character and fully justified why they think it would be a challenge to portray – 2 marks
- Has identified the character and given some justification as to why they think it would be a challenge to portray – 1 mark

Candidates may include some of the following as reasons: social, economic, cultural background, personality, status, physical appearance, relationship with other characters, voice and movement.

Answer should be from the point of view of an actor.

A full justification will give two reasons for choice.

Some justification would be one reason.

(b) Candidates are asked to describe a relationship between the character they answered on in question 4(a) and one other character in their drama.

Two marks for fully describing the relationship.

One mark for adequately describing the relationship.

Relationships between characters can be described in a number of ways. Candidates should make reference to:

1. What the specific relationship is (mother/daughter, friendship, husband/wife, teacher/pupil etc).

AND

Candidates may also make reference to:

2. How they know one another (work, school etc)

3. How long have they known one another (just met, many years)?

4. How they feel about one another (enjoy one another's company, despise one another).

(c) Candidates are asked to explain two activities they would do to establish and/or develop this in rehearsals.

Two marks for each rehearsal activity used to establish and/or develop this relationship with reason.

Although candidates might choose from a wide range of activities, good answers will show an understanding of the characterisation process. Activities described could, for example, include improvisation, research, hot seating, thought tunnel, thought tracking or techniques. It is not sufficient to describe in general terms discussing and rehearsing.

The candidate:

- Has fully explained two or more appropriate practical drama activities, with a detailed explanation of how they would contribute to the establishment and/or development of this relationship – 4 marks

- Has adequately explained two or more appropriate practical drama activities, with an adequate explanation of how they would contribute to the establishment and/or development of this relationship – 3 marks

- Has partially explained two or more practical drama activities, and may have given some indication of how they would contribute to the establishment and/or development of this relationship.

There are two marks for each activity described (max two activities). Where candidates have explained more than two activities, the best two will be marked.

EXAMPLES

Rehearsed improvisation: allows the director to help the actors deepen their understanding of their characters as they can explore what they understand about the characters and character relationships outwith the confines of the drama.

Hot seating: asking the character questions, using the correct vocal and movement techniques for the character. Helps explore physicality or how to "play" a character and with character relationships, developing personality, background, understanding objectives etc.

5. (a) Candidates are asked to describe a key moment in their drama with justification.

Four marks are available for the question.

Candidates may give a full and detailed description of the key moment and two reasons why they think this

OR

Candidates may give an adequate description of the key moment and three reasons why they think this.

(b) Candidates are asked to describe how they would use two production areas to highlight/enhance their key moment. They should give two examples with reasons.

Three marks for describing how each production area would highlight/enhance this key moment.

EXAMPLE

Sound — to build tension, create mood/atmosphere, give feeling of period, give feeling of style (Western, love story), appropriate sound effect making drama more realistic.

Lighting — give appropriate mood/atmosphere, more realistic, focus attention of audience, build tension.

Props — dress the set, add to the realism, help the characters believe in what they are doing, help set the time period, help to enhance where the scene is set.

Set — more realistic, help staging, create sense of period, create atmosphere/mood, create tension.

Costume — more realistic, tie in with theme, help set scene, time period, simplify characters etc.

Make-up — more realistic, make characters stand out, help to highlight death scene, set time period, build tension.

Candidates may choose to give a full explanation with reason or an adequate explanation with two reasons. Either is acceptable as long as the idea is practicable.

One mark for what they would do and two marks for reasons why this would have highlighted/enhanced it.

OR

Two marks for what they would do and one mark for reason why this would have highlighted/enhanced it.

NATIONAL 5 DRAMA MODEL PAPER 1

Section 1

1. (a) Candidates are asked to describe the main problem they had during preparation for their performance. Two marks for fully explained problem.

   2

   (b) Two marks for fully explained solution of the problem given in (a).

   2

2. Candidates are asked to evaluate their final performance and impact on the audience. Answer may include comments on:

   • Acting — performance concept, voice, movement, blocking, mood and atmosphere, impact on the audience.

   • Lighting — design concept, mood and atmosphere, operation, use of resources and impact on the audience.

   • Sound — design concept, mood and atmosphere, operation, use of resources and impact on the audience.

   • Costume — design concept, effectiveness, use of resources and impact on the audience.

   • Make-up — design concept, effectiveness, use of resources and impact on the audience.

   • Set — design concept, effectiveness, use of resources and impact on the audience.

   • Props — design concept, effectiveness, use of resources and impact on the audience.

   6

Section 2

3. (a) There are 2 marks for suggesting and justifying a target audience for the drama.

   A full justification will give two reasons for choice — 2 marks. Some justification would be one reason — 1 mark. All are acceptable but answers should be positive **not** negative.

   2

   (b) The candidate should give justified comments about how the audience chosen in (a) might respond to their drama with one or more appropriate emotional reaction(s):

   • Detailed and fully justified comments — 4 marks

   • Adequate and some justified comments — 2–3 marks

   • Limited and partial justified comments — 0–1 mark

   4

4. (a) Candidates should state the character they feel the target audience would react strongly to, justifying their choice. A full justification will give two reasons for choice — 2 marks. Some justification would be one reason — 1 mark.

   2

(b) Candidates should explain why they think their target audience would react strongly to this character. Marks should not be awarded for mere descriptive comments.

- Detailed and fully justified comments — 4 marks
- Adequate and some justified comments — 2–3 marks
- Limited and partial justified comments — 0–1 mark

Candidates may refer to a range of relevant reasons such as personality, relationships, role/purpose in the drama, exemplification of the theme/issue, emotional reactions, age, comic/tragic value etc.

4

5. (a) Candidates are asked to describe an important moment in their drama with justification, which contains the character from their previous answer.

4

(b) Candidates should give at least two examples with reasons. One to three marks for describing how each production area would emphasise this important moment.

- Sound — to build tension, create mood/atmosphere, give feeling of period, give feeling of style (horror, comedy etc.), appropriate sound effect making drama more realistic.
- Lighting — give appropriate mood/atmosphere, more realistic, focus attention of audience, build tension.
- Props — dress the set, add to the realism, help the characters believe in what they are doing, help set the time period, help to enhance where the scene is set.
- Set — more realistic, help staging, create sense of period, create atmosphere/mood, create tension.
- Costume — more realistic, tie in with theme, help set scene, time period, simplify characters etc.
- Make-up — more realistic, make characters stand out, help to highlight death scene, set time period, build tension.

Must link to the important key moment. Candidates may choose to give a full explanation with reason or an adequate explanation with two reasons. Either is acceptable as long as the idea is practicable.

6

6. (a) Purpose: the answer might refer for example to what a character has to do in the drama, impact on the audience, highlighting theme or message, mood, atmosphere, characters, relationships, period, setting etc. They should explain how their purpose highlights the low status of the chosen character.

2

(b) Candidates could refer to any voice direction that would help the actor highlight the low status of the character. Reference may be made to pace, pitch, tone, volume, intonation, clarity, fluency, accent, register.

3

(c) Candidates could refer to any movement direction that would help the actor highlight the low status of the character. Reference may be made to use of space, gesture, body language, positioning, facial expression, eye contact, posture.

3

NATIONAL 5 DRAMA MODEL PAPER 2

Section 1

1. Candidates are asked to choose a target audience from two examples. Two marks for fully justified explanation of which audience they would choose.

2. One mark each for fully explained problem and one mark each for fully explained solution of the problems given.

3. Candidates are asked to describe two changes they would make to their contribution to the final performance. Answer may include comments on:

- Acting — performance concept, voice, movement, blocking, mood and atmosphere, impact on the audience.
- Lighting — design concept, mood and atmosphere, operation, use of resources and impact on the audience.
- Sound — design concept, mood and atmosphere, operation, use of resources and impact on the audience.
- Costume — design concept, effectiveness, use of resources and impact on the audience.
- Make up — design concept, effectiveness, use of resources and impact on the audience.
- Set — design concept, effectiveness, use of resources and impact on the audience.
- Props — design concept, effectiveness, use of resources and impact on the audience.

4

Section 2

4. For four marks the candidate should: give a clear, concise outline of the dramatic presentation. Details of the time and place are clearly stated.

4

5. (a) A mood and/or atmosphere should be given but will not be credited. A full and clear justification for 4 marks should be given for the mood and atmosphere in the opening scene. Detailed and fully justified comments — 4 marks.

4

(b) They should give at least two examples with reasons. One to three marks for describing how each production area would create this mood/atmosphere:

- Sound — volume, to build tension, create mood/atmosphere, give feeling of period, give feeling of genre (horror, comedy etc.), appropriate sound effect making drama more realistic
- Lighting — give appropriate mood/atmosphere, use of gels for wash, intensity, use of blackouts, focus attention of audience, build tension
- Props — dress the set, add to the realism, help the characters believe in what they are doing, help set the time period, help to enhance where the scene is set, use of pre-set and/or personal props
- Set — more realistic, help staging, create sense of period, create atmosphere/mood, create tension

- Costume — more realistic, tie in with theme, help set scene, time period, simplify characters etc.
- Make-up — more realistic, make characters stand out, help to highlight death scene, set time period, build tension

If only one mentioned mark out of three.

Must link to the mood/atmosphere mentioned. Candidates may choose to give a full explanation with reason or an adequate explanation with two reasons. Either is acceptable as long as the idea is practicable.

6

. (a) Candidate gives full and detailed account of the conflict and/or tension in their drama.

2

(b) Candidate may refer to how they would use practical drama techniques or other appropriate theatrical means to demonstrate the conflict and/or tension. Reference may be made to use of tableau work, hot-seating, improvisation/role play, focusing on certain scenes/characters, use of role reversal etc.

4

7. (a) Two marks are available for outlining what we learn about the character's personality from the candidate's drama.

A further two marks are available for explaining that character's function or purpose in the drama. Answers might refer, for example, to the action, imparting information, use of dramatic irony, building tension, mood and atmosphere, characters and relationships, highlighting a theme etc.

4

(b) Candidate may make reference to appropriate voice and movement to highlight character's personality as described in (a). They may also refer to aspects of theatre arts such as costume use of personal props.

Two aspects on voice or movement, if detailed enough, is sufficient however for four marks.

6

NATIONAL 5 DRAMA
MODEL PAPER 3

Section 1

1. Two marks for a full explanation of how their role improved the overall performance.

2

2. Two marks for stating if they were successful in their role. A candidate may state that they were not successful which is equally as valid as long as it is fully justified.

2

3. Two marks are given for a full and clear description of the moment. If candidate describes a scene they will gain no credit for this part to the answer. Four marks are given for how their role achieved this. This part of the answer may include comments on:

- Acting — performance concept, voice, movement, blocking, mood and atmosphere, impact on the audience.
- Lighting — design concept, mood and atmosphere, operation, use of resources and impact on the audience.
- Sound — design concept, mood and atmosphere, operation, use of resources and impact on the audience.
- Costume — design concept, effectiveness, use of resources and impact on the audience.
- Make-up — design concept, effectiveness, use of resources and impact on the audience.
- Set — design concept, effectiveness, use of resources and impact on the audience.
- Props — design concept, effectiveness, use of resources and impact on the audience.

6

Section 2

4. One mark for a recognisable form.   **1**

5. (a) A full and clear description for four marks should be given with reference made to appropriate set, flats, rostra, trucks, projections on cyclorama etc. The candidate may also refer to the height and colour of the set.

4

(b) This question should be marked holistically. The question specifically asks the candidate to detail how at least two theatre arts from the list can be used to make the SET clear and interesting so responses must be linked back to question 5(a).

If less than two theatre arts are discussed a maximum of three marks for this question should be awarded.

6

6. (a) Candidates should give a clear purpose of their main character for the two marks. If candidate states role no marks should be awarded.

2

(b) Candidates should state clearly how the main character could be communicated to the audience. Reference may be made to voice and movement, theatre arts, status with other characters, actor/audience relationship, other character relationships, role/purpose in the drama, exemplification of the theme/issue, emotional reactions, etc.

6

7. (a) Candidates are asked to describe how their final scene could be turned into a tableau. Mark holistically. Candidates may refer to facial expression, body language, gesture, use of levels and space, positioning, setting.

6

(b) Candidates must state whether a tableau would be successful or not; however, full marks are given for the justification. A clear and appropriate justification will gain two marks. A vague justification and/or not appropriate justification will credit zero to one mark.

3

2

8. Genre could be comedy, tragedy, tragic-comedy, horror, romantic or any other valid genre for production.

Candidate should give at least two examples with reasons. 1-3 marks for describing how each production area would highlight the genre.

- SOUND — to build tension, create mood/atmosphere, give feeling of period, give feeling of genre (tragedy, horror, comedy etc.), appropriate sound effect
- LIGHTING — Give appropriate mood/atmosphere, more realistic, focus attention of audience, use of colour, gels
- PROPS — Dress the set, personal props, add to the realism, help the characters believe in what they are doing, help set the time period, help to enhance where the scene is set
- SET — More realistic, help staging, create sense of period, create atmosphere/mood, colour, height, create tension
- COSTUME — More realistic, tie in with theme, help set scene, time period, simplify characters etc.
- MAKE UP — More realistic, make characters stand out, help to highlight death scene, set time period, use of specific make-up such as fake blood or exaggerated make-up

Must link to the genre. Candidates may choose to give a full explanation with reason or an adequate explanation with two reasons. Either is acceptable as long as the idea is practicable.

6

NATIONAL 5 DRAMA 2014

Overview
National 5 level candidates are required to demonstrate knowledge and understanding of both process and performance.

Section 1 is designed to test the candidates' ability to evaluate their own and others' work. Section 2 tests the candidates' ability to respond to stimuli and create their own piece of drama.

Section 1
These questions require candidates to give a personal evaluative response to a piece of work they have been involved in during the course. This may be from the Drama Skills or Production Units or from the Course Assessment Performance.

The questions require candidates to demonstrate their reflection and evaluation skills.

Section 2
Candidates are required to demonstrate knowledge and understanding of creating drama by responding to stimuli. The questions should be suitable for candidates with a relatively detailed knowledge as well as those whose knowledge is more wide ranging.

Section 1

1. (a) Candidates are asked to select the scene which they thought was the most challenging. Must give a brief description for the mark.

   (b) The candidate has fully explained why they thought this scene was the most challenging for two marks.

   (c) The candidate gives a full and detailed solution as to how they overcame the challenge(s) or two adequate solutions for two marks.

   (d) Answer may include comments/sketches/drawings/notes on:

   Acting – performance concept, voice, movement, blocking, characterisation techniques.

   Lighting – design concept, use of resources.

   Sound – design concept, use of resources.

   Costume – design concept, use of resources.

   Make up – design concept, use of resources.

   Set – design concept, use of resources.

   Props – design concept, use of resources.

Section 2

2. There is 1 mark for identifying the target audience and 1 mark for justifying an ideal target audience for the drama.

3. The candidate has given a full and detailed explanation about the type of drama the audience would see. Correct terminology must be used.

4. (a) Candidate is asked to state a theme or issue. 1 mark awarded for any valid response.

   (b) Candidate should make a statement showing how the theme or issue they have stated in Q4(a) is developed for two marks.

   The candidate has given a full and detailed description of how they would develop the theme or issue.

(c) Candidate must discuss at least two characters for three marks. Candidate response must show the character's thoughts/feelings in reference to the theme/issue stated in Q4(a).

The candidate has given a full and detailed explanation of how they would highlight the theme/issue through character relationships. If only one character described award zero marks.

. (a) Candidates should state the chosen character from their drama and explain their purpose.

The candidate has clearly identified one character and has fully explained their purpose in the drama.

(b) Answers must explain how the character discussed in question Q5(a) feels about one other character from their drama:

The candidate has made full and detailed justified comments about how their chosen character feels about one other character in their drama.

. (a) Candidates should give a brief description of a key moment in their drama and provide a reason for this.

The candidate has clearly identified a moment in their drama which is important with relevant justification.

(b) Candidates could refer to any voice or movement direction that would help the actors highlight the moment identified in Q6(a).

Candidates may choose to give any combination of voice and movement direction –

3 voice and 1 movement
2 voice and 2 movement
1 voice and 3 movement

All are acceptable. Answer must be from the point of view of a character or zero marks will be awarded. Correct terminology should be used.

(c) Candidates should select two production skills from the list (Costume, Make up, Props or Lighting) and explain how they would help to highlight the key moment from Q6(a).

Three marks for explaining how each production area would highlight this key moment.

COSTUME – More realistic, tie in with theme, help set scene, time period, simplify characters, etc.

MAKE UP – More realistic, make characters stand out, set time period, build tension, etc.

PROPS – Dress the set, add to the realism, help the characters believe in what they are doing, help set the time period, help to enhance where the scene is set, etc.

LIGHTING – Give appropriate mood/atmosphere, more realistic, focus attention of audience, build tension, etc.

Acknowledgements

Permission has been sought from all relevant copyright holders and Hodder Gibson is grateful for the use of the following:

The photograph 'Where childhood memories go?' by Carlos Chacon, taken from www.Charlie.cr.smugmug.com. Reproduced by permission of Carlos Chacon (SQP page 4);

An extract from "Passing Places' copyright © 1990 Stephen Greenhorn. Excerpted with permission of Nick Hern Books Ltd: www.nickhernbooks.co.uk (SQP page 5);

An excerpt from "The Center of Attention' by Daniel Hoffman, published by Random House. Copyright © 1970 by Daniel Hoffman (Model Paper 1 page 4);

A Scottish saying © Geddes MacGregor (Model Paper 1 page 4);

An extract from 'The Lewis Man' by Peter May, published by Quercus Books, 2012 (Model Paper 2 page 4);

An extract from 'Sparkleshark' by Philip Ridley, published by Samuel French Ltd, 2000 (ISBN 978-0573051227) (Model Paper 2 page 5);

An extract from 'Dunsinane' © David Greig and reprinted by permission of Faber and Faber Ltd (Model Paper 3 page 5);

Image © Dundanim/Shutterstock.com (2014 page 6);

An extract from 'Medea' copyright © 2000 Liz Lochhead. Excerpted with permission of Nick Hern Books Ltd: www.nickhernbooks.co.uk (2014 page 6).

Hodder Gibson would like to thank SQA for use of any past exam questions that may have been used in model papers, whether amended or in original form.